The Natural Magic Journal

A Daily Practice
for Clarity and Creativity

First published by Phoenix & Kelpie Press 2025
Copyright © Elle Hartford 2025

ISBN: 979-8-9921588-2-3

Welcome to your new journal!

Don't be afraid to make these pages your own. You might use the box outlines for sketches or stickers, or for tarot cards, or even words of the day; likewise, the circle outline could be the moon phase, a map, or space for yet more stickers. The possibilities are endless! If only the pages were, too . . .

Journal Author:

_____

Journal Intention:

_____

_____

_____

_____

Date:

Location:

In a Nutshell: _____

_____

_____

More Details: _____

_____

_____

_____

_____

_____

_____

_____

Date:
Location:

In a Nutshell: _____

_____

_____

More Details: _____

_____

_____

_____

_____

_____

_____

_____

Date:

Location:

In a Nutshell: _____

_____

_____

More Details: _____

_____

_____

_____

_____

_____

_____

_____

Date:
Location:

In a Nutshell: _____

_____

_____

More Details: _____

_____

_____

_____

_____

_____

_____

_____

Date:
Location:

In a Nutshell: _____

_____

_____

More Details: _____

_____

_____

_____

_____

_____

_____

_____

Date:
Location:

In a Nutshell: _____

_____

_____

More Details: _____

_____

_____

_____

_____

_____

_____

_____

Date:

Location:

In a Nutshell: _____

_____

_____

More Details: _____

_____

_____

_____

_____

_____

_____

_____

_____

Date:
Location:

In a Nutshell: _____

_____

_____

More Details: _____

_____

_____

_____

_____

_____

_____

_____

_____

Date:
Location:

In a Nutshell: _____

_____

_____

More Details: _____

_____

_____

_____

_____

_____

_____

_____

Date:
Location:

In a Nutshell: _____

_____

_____

More Details: _____

_____

_____

_____

_____

_____

_____

_____

Date:
Location:

In a Nutshell: _____

_____

_____

More Details: _____

_____

_____

_____

_____

_____

_____

_____

_____

Date:
Location:

In a Nutshell: _____

_____

_____

More Details: _____

_____

_____

_____

_____

_____

_____

_____

Date:
Location:

In a Nutshell: _____

_____

_____

More Details: _____

_____

_____

_____

_____

_____

_____

_____

_____

Date:
Location:

In a Nutshell: _____

_____

_____

More Details: _____

_____

_____

_____

_____

_____

_____

_____

Date:

Location:

In a Nutshell: _____

_____

_____

More Details: _____

_____

_____

_____

_____

_____

_____

_____

Date:
Location:

In a Nutshell: _____

_____

_____

More Details: _____

_____

_____

_____

_____

_____

_____

_____

Date:

Location:

In a Nutshell: _____

_____

_____

More Details: _____

_____

_____

_____

_____

_____

_____

_____

Date:
Location:

In a Nutshell: _____
_____
_____

More Details: _____
_____
_____
_____
_____
_____
_____
_____
_____

Date:

Location:

In a Nutshell: _____

_____

_____

More Details: _____

_____

_____

_____

_____

_____

_____

_____

_____

Date:
Location:

In a Nutshell: _____

_____

_____

More Details: _____

_____

_____

_____

_____

_____

_____

_____

Date:

Location:

In a Nutshell: _____

_____

_____

More Details: _____

_____

_____

_____

_____

_____

_____

_____

_____

Date:
Location:

In a Nutshell: _____

_____

_____

More Details: _____

_____

_____

_____

_____

_____

_____

_____

Date:
Location:

In a Nutshell: _____

_____

_____

More Details: _____

_____

_____

_____

_____

_____

_____

_____

_____

Date:
Location:

In a Nutshell: _____

_____

_____

More Details: _____

_____

_____

_____

_____

_____

_____

_____

_____

Date:
Location:

In a Nutshell: _____
_____
_____

More Details: _____
_____
_____
_____
_____
_____
_____
_____
_____

Date:
Location:

In a Nutshell: _____

_____

_____

More Details: _____

_____

_____

_____

_____

_____

_____

_____

Date:
Location:

In a Nutshell: _____
_____
_____

More Details: _____
_____
_____
_____
_____
_____
_____
_____

Date:
Location:

In a Nutshell: _____
_____
_____

More Details: _____
_____
_____
_____
_____
_____
_____
_____
_____

Date:
Location:

In a Nutshell: _____

_____

_____

More Details: _____

_____

_____

_____

_____

_____

_____

_____

Date:

Location:

In a Nutshell: _____

_____

_____

More Details: _____

_____

_____

_____

_____

_____

_____

_____

_____

Date:
Location:

In a Nutshell: _____

_____

_____

More Details: _____

_____

_____

_____

_____

_____

_____

_____

Date:
Location:

In a Nutshell: _____

_____

_____

More Details: _____

_____

_____

_____

_____

_____

_____

_____

Date:
Location:

In a Nutshell: _____

_____

_____

More Details: _____

_____

_____

_____

_____

_____

_____

_____

Date:
Location:

In a Nutshell: _____

_____

_____

More Details: _____

_____

_____

_____

_____

_____

_____

_____

Date:
Location:

In a Nutshell: _____
_____
_____

More Details: _____
_____
_____
_____
_____
_____
_____
_____
_____

Date:

Location:

In a Nutshell: _____

_____

_____

More Details: _____

_____

_____

_____

_____

_____

_____

_____

_____

Date:
Location:

In a Nutshell: _____
_____
_____

More Details: _____
_____
_____
_____
_____
_____
_____
_____
_____

Date:
Location:

In a Nutshell: _____
_____
_____

More Details: _____
_____
_____
_____
_____
_____
_____
_____
_____

Date:
Location:

In a Nutshell: _____

_____

_____

More Details: _____

_____

_____

_____

_____

_____

_____

_____

_____

Date:
Location:

In a Nutshell: _____

_____

_____

More Details: _____

_____

_____

_____

_____

_____

_____

_____

Date:
Location:

In a Nutshell: _____

_____

_____

More Details: _____

_____

_____

_____

_____

_____

_____

_____

Date:
Location:

In a Nutshell: _____

_____

_____

More Details: _____

_____

_____

_____

_____

_____

_____

_____

_____

Date:
Location:

In a Nutshell: _____
_____
_____

More Details: _____
_____
_____
_____
_____
_____
_____
_____

Date:
Location:

In a Nutshell: _____

_____

_____

More Details: _____

_____

_____

_____

_____

_____

_____

_____

_____

Date:

Location:

In a Nutshell: _____

_____

_____

More Details: _____

_____

_____

_____

_____

_____

_____

_____

Date:
Location:

In a Nutshell: _____

_____

_____

More Details: _____

_____

_____

_____

_____

_____

_____

_____

Date:

Location:

In a Nutshell: _____

_____

_____

More Details: _____

_____

_____

_____

_____

_____

_____

_____

_____

Date:
Location:

In a Nutshell: _____

_____

_____

More Details: _____

_____

_____

_____

_____

_____

_____

_____

_____

Date:

Location:

In a Nutshell: _____

_____

_____

More Details: _____

_____

_____

_____

_____

_____

_____

_____

Date:
Location:

In a Nutshell: _____

_____

_____

More Details: _____

_____

_____

_____

_____

_____

_____

_____

Date:
Location:

In a Nutshell: _____

_____

_____

More Details: _____

_____

_____

_____

_____

_____

_____

_____

Date:
Location:

In a Nutshell: _____

_____

_____

More Details: _____

_____

_____

_____

_____

_____

_____

_____

Date:
Location:

In a Nutshell: _____

_____

_____

More Details: _____

_____

_____

_____

_____

_____

_____

_____

Date:
Location:

In a Nutshell: _____

_____

_____

More Details: _____

_____

_____

_____

_____

_____

_____

_____

Date:
Location:

In a Nutshell: _____

_____

_____

More Details: _____

_____

_____

_____

_____

_____

_____

_____

Date:
Location:

In a Nutshell: _____

_____

_____

More Details: _____

_____

_____

_____

_____

_____

_____

_____

Date:
Location:

In a Nutshell: _____

_____

_____

More Details: _____

_____

_____

_____

_____

_____

_____

_____

Date:
Location:

In a Nutshell: _____

_____

_____

More Details: _____

_____

_____

_____

_____

_____

_____

_____

Date:
Location:

In a Nutshell: _____

_____

_____

More Details: _____

_____

_____

_____

_____

_____

_____

_____

Date:

Location:

In a Nutshell: _____

_____

_____

More Details: _____

_____

_____

_____

_____

_____

_____

_____

_____

Date:

Location:

In a Nutshell: _____

_____

_____

More Details: _____

_____

_____

_____

_____

_____

_____

_____

Date:
Location:

In a Nutshell: _____

_____

_____

More Details: _____

_____

_____

_____

_____

_____

_____

_____

Date:
Location:

In a Nutshell: _____

_____

_____

More Details: _____

_____

_____

_____

_____

_____

_____

_____

Date:
Location:

In a Nutshell: _____
_____
_____

More Details: _____
_____
_____
_____
_____
_____
_____
_____
_____

Date:
Location:

In a Nutshell: _____

_____

_____

More Details: _____

_____

_____

_____

_____

_____

_____

_____

Date:

Location:

In a Nutshell: _____

_____

_____

More Details: _____

_____

_____

_____

_____

_____

_____

_____

Date:
Location:

In a Nutshell: _____

_____

_____

More Details: _____

_____

_____

_____

_____

_____

_____

_____

Date:
Location:

In a Nutshell: _____
_____
_____

More Details: _____
_____
_____
_____
_____
_____
_____
_____

Date:
Location:

In a Nutshell: _____

_____

_____

More Details: _____

_____

_____

_____

_____

_____

_____

_____

Date:
Location:

In a Nutshell: _____
_____
_____

More Details: _____
_____
_____
_____
_____
_____
_____
_____

Date:
Location:

In a Nutshell: _____
_____
_____

More Details: _____
_____
_____
_____
_____
_____
_____
_____

Date:
Location:

In a Nutshell: _____

_____

_____

More Details: _____

_____

_____

_____

_____

_____

_____

_____

Date:
Location:

In a Nutshell: _____

_____

_____

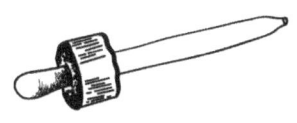

More Details: _____

_____

_____

_____

_____

_____

_____

_____

Date:
Location:

In a Nutshell: _____

_____

_____

More Details: _____

_____

_____

_____

_____

_____

_____

_____

_____

Date:
Location:

In a Nutshell: _____
_____
_____

More Details: _____
_____
_____
_____
_____
_____
_____
_____
_____

Date:
Location:

In a Nutshell: _____

_____

_____

More Details: _____

_____

_____

_____

_____

_____

_____

_____

Date:
Location:

In a Nutshell: _____

_____

_____

More Details: _____

_____

_____

_____

_____

_____

_____

_____

Date:
Location:

In a Nutshell: _____

_____

_____

More Details: _____

_____

_____

_____

_____

_____

_____

_____

Date:

Location:

In a Nutshell: _____

_____

_____

More Details: _____

_____

_____

_____

_____

_____

_____

_____

Date:
Location:

In a Nutshell: _____

_____

_____

More Details: _____

_____

_____

_____

_____

_____

_____

_____

_____

Date:

Location:

In a Nutshell: _____

_____

_____

More Details: _____

_____

_____

_____

_____

_____

_____

_____

Date:
Location:

In a Nutshell: _____
_____
_____

More Details: _____
_____
_____
_____
_____
_____
_____
_____

Date:

Location:

In a Nutshell: _____

_____

_____

More Details: _____

_____

_____

_____

_____

_____

_____

_____

Date:
Location:

In a Nutshell: _____

_____

_____

More Details: _____

_____

_____

_____

_____

_____

_____

_____

Date:
Location:

In a Nutshell: _____

_____

_____

More Details: _____

_____

_____

_____

_____

_____

_____

_____

Date:
Location:

In a Nutshell: _____

_____

_____

More Details: _____

_____

_____

_____

_____

_____

_____

_____

Date:
Location:

In a Nutshell: _____

_____

_____

More Details: _____

_____

_____

_____

_____

_____

_____

_____

Date:
Location:

In a Nutshell: _____

_____

_____

More Details: _____

_____

_____

_____

_____

_____

_____

_____

Date:
Location:

In a Nutshell: _____

_____

_____

More Details: _____

_____

_____

_____

_____

_____

_____

_____

_____

_____

Date:
Location:

In a Nutshell: _____

_____

_____

More Details: _____

_____

_____

_____

_____

_____

_____

_____

Date:
Location:

In a Nutshell: _____

_____

_____

More Details: _____

_____

_____

_____

_____

_____

_____

_____

Date:
Location:

In a Nutshell: _____

_____

_____

More Details: _____

_____

_____

_____

_____

_____

_____

_____

Date:
Location:

In a Nutshell: _____

_____

_____

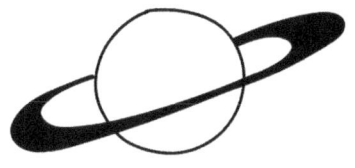

More Details: _____

_____

_____

_____

_____

_____

_____

_____

Date:
Location:

In a Nutshell: _____

_____

_____

More Details: _____

_____

_____

_____

_____

_____

_____

_____

Date:
Location:

In a Nutshell: _____

_____

_____

More Details: _____

_____

_____

_____

_____

_____

_____

_____

Date:

Location:

In a Nutshell: _____

_____

_____

More Details: _____

_____

_____

_____

_____

_____

_____

_____

Date:
Location:

In a Nutshell: _____

_____

_____

More Details: _____

_____

_____

_____

_____

_____

_____

_____

Date:
Location:

In a Nutshell: _____
_____
_____

More Details: _____
_____
_____
_____
_____
_____
_____
_____

Date:
Location:

In a Nutshell: _____

_____

_____

More Details: _____

_____

_____

_____

_____

_____

_____

_____

_____

Date:

Location:

In a Nutshell: _____

_____

_____

More Details: _____

_____

_____

_____

_____

_____

_____

_____

Date:
Location:

In a Nutshell: _____

_____

_____

More Details: _____

_____

_____

_____

_____

_____

_____

_____

Date:
Location:

In a Nutshell: _____

_____

_____

More Details: _____

_____

_____

_____

_____

_____

_____

_____

_____

Date:
Location:

In a Nutshell: _____

_____

_____

More Details: _____

_____

_____

_____

_____

_____

_____

_____

Date:
Location:

In a Nutshell: _____

_____

_____

More Details: _____

_____

_____

_____

_____

_____

_____

_____

Date:
Location:

In a Nutshell: _____

_____

_____

More Details: _____

_____

_____

_____

_____

_____

_____

_____

Date:
Location:

In a Nutshell: _____

_____

_____

More Details: _____

_____

_____

_____

_____

_____

_____

_____

Date:

Location:

In a Nutshell: _____

_____

_____

More Details: _____

_____

_____

_____

_____

_____

_____

_____

_____

Date:
Location:

In a Nutshell: _____

_____

_____

More Details: _____

_____

_____

_____

_____

_____

_____

_____

Date:
Location:

In a Nutshell: _____

_____

_____

More Details: _____

_____

_____

_____

_____

_____

_____

_____

Date:

Location:

In a Nutshell: _____

_____

_____

More Details: _____

_____

_____

_____

_____

_____

_____

_____

_____

Date:
Location:

In a Nutshell: _____
_____
_____

More Details: _____
_____
_____
_____
_____
_____
_____
_____

Date:
Location:

In a Nutshell: _____

_____

_____

More Details: _____

_____

_____

_____

_____

_____

_____

_____

Date:
Location:

In a Nutshell: _____
_____
_____

More Details: _____
_____
_____
_____
_____
_____
_____
_____

Date:
Location:

In a Nutshell: _____

_____

_____

More Details: _____

_____

_____

_____

_____

_____

_____

_____

Date:
Location:

In a Nutshell: _____

_____

_____

More Details: _____

_____

_____

_____

_____

_____

_____

_____

Date:
Location:

In a Nutshell: _____

_____

_____

More Details: _____

_____

_____

_____

_____

_____

_____

_____

Date:
Location:

In a Nutshell: _____
_____
_____

More Details: _____
_____
_____
_____
_____
_____
_____
_____
_____

Date:
Location:

In a Nutshell: _____

_____

_____

More Details: _____

_____

_____

_____

_____

_____

_____

_____

_____

Date:

Location:

In a Nutshell: _____

_____

_____

More Details: _____

_____

_____

_____

_____

_____

_____

_____

Date:

Location:

In a Nutshell: _____

_____

_____

More Details: _____

_____

_____

_____

_____

_____

_____

_____

_____

Date:
Location:

In a Nutshell: _____

_____

_____

More Details: _____

_____

_____

_____

_____

_____

_____

_____

Date:
Location:

In a Nutshell: _____

_____

_____

More Details: _____

_____

_____

_____

_____

_____

_____

_____

_____

Date:
Location:

In a Nutshell: _____
_____
_____

More Details: _____
_____
_____
_____
_____
_____
_____
_____
_____

Date:
Location:

In a Nutshell: _____

_____

_____

More Details: _____

_____

_____

_____

_____

_____

_____

_____

Date:
Location:

In a Nutshell: _____

_____

_____

More Details: _____

_____

_____

_____

_____

_____

_____

_____

Date:
Location:

In a Nutshell: _____

_____

_____

More Details: _____

_____

_____

_____

_____

_____

_____

_____

Date:
Location:

In a Nutshell: _____

_____

_____

More Details: _____

_____

_____

_____

_____

_____

_____

_____

Date:
Location:

In a Nutshell: _____
_____
_____

More Details: _____
_____
_____
_____
_____
_____
_____
_____
_____

Date:
Location:

In a Nutshell: _____
_____
_____

More Details: _____
_____
_____
_____
_____
_____
_____
_____
_____

Date:

Location:

In a Nutshell: _____

_____

_____

More Details: _____

_____

_____

_____

_____

_____

_____

_____

_____

Date:
Location:

In a Nutshell: _____

_____

_____

More Details: _____

_____

_____

_____

_____

_____

_____

_____

_____

Date:

Location:

In a Nutshell: _____

_____

_____

More Details: _____

_____

_____

_____

_____

_____

_____

_____

_____

Date:

Location:

In a Nutshell: _____

_____

_____

More Details: _____

_____

_____

_____

_____

_____

_____

_____

_____

Date:
Location:

In a Nutshell: _____

_____

_____

More Details: _____

_____

_____

_____

_____

_____

_____

_____

Date:

Location:

In a Nutshell: _____

_____

_____

More Details: _____

_____

_____

_____

_____

_____

_____

_____

_____

Date:
Location:

In a Nutshell: _____

_____

_____

More Details: _____

_____

_____

_____

_____

_____

_____

_____

Date:
Location:

In a Nutshell: _____
_____
_____

More Details: _____
_____
_____
_____
_____
_____
_____
_____

Date:
Location:

In a Nutshell: _____

_____

_____

More Details: _____

_____

_____

_____

_____

_____

_____

_____

Date:
Location:

In a Nutshell: _____

_____

_____

More Details: _____

_____

_____

_____

_____

_____

_____

_____

Date:

Location:

In a Nutshell: _____

_____

_____

More Details: _____

_____

_____

_____

_____

_____

_____

_____

_____

Date:
Location:

In a Nutshell: _____

_____

_____

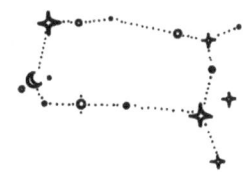

More Details: _____

_____

_____

_____

_____

_____

_____

_____

Date:
Location:

In a Nutshell: _____

_____

_____

More Details: _____

_____

_____

_____

_____

_____

_____

_____

Date:
Location:

In a Nutshell: _____

_____

_____

More Details: _____

_____

_____

_____

_____

_____

_____

_____

Date:
Location:

In a Nutshell: _____
_____
_____

More Details: _____
_____
_____
_____
_____
_____
_____
_____

Date:
Location:

In a Nutshell: _____

_____

_____

More Details: _____

_____

_____

_____

_____

_____

_____

_____

Date:
Location:

In a Nutshell: _____

_____

_____

More Details: _____

_____

_____

_____

_____

_____

_____

_____

Date:
Location:

In a Nutshell: _____

_____

_____

More Details: _____

_____

_____

_____

_____

_____

_____

_____

Date:
Location:

In a Nutshell: _____

_____

_____

More Details: _____

_____

_____

_____

_____

_____

_____

_____

Date:

Location:

In a Nutshell: _____

_____

_____

More Details: _____

_____

_____

_____

_____

_____

_____

_____

_____

Date:
Location:

In a Nutshell: _____
_____
_____

More Details: _____
_____
_____
_____
_____
_____
_____
_____

Date:
Location:

In a Nutshell: _____

_____

_____

More Details: _____

_____

_____

_____

_____

_____

_____

_____

Date:
Location:

In a Nutshell: _____
_____
_____

More Details: _____
_____
_____
_____
_____
_____
_____
_____

Date:
Location:

In a Nutshell: _____

_____

_____

More Details: _____

_____

_____

_____

_____

_____

_____

_____

Date:

Location:

In a Nutshell: _____

_____

_____

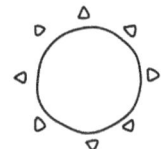

More Details: _____

_____

_____

_____

_____

_____

_____

_____

Date:
Location:

In a Nutshell: _____

_____

_____

More Details: _____

_____

_____

_____

_____

_____

_____

_____

Date:

Location:

In a Nutshell: _____

_____

_____

More Details: _____

_____

_____

_____

_____

_____

_____

_____

Date:
Location:

In a Nutshell: _____
_____
_____

More Details: _____
_____
_____
_____
_____
_____
_____
_____
_____

Date:
Location:

In a Nutshell: _____

_____

_____

More Details: _____

_____

_____

_____

_____

_____

_____

_____

Date:
Location:

In a Nutshell: _____
_____
_____

More Details: _____
_____
_____
_____
_____
_____
_____
_____
_____

Date:
Location:

In a Nutshell: _____
_____
_____

More Details: _____
_____
_____
_____
_____
_____
_____
_____

Date:

Location:

In a Nutshell: _____

_____

_____

More Details: _____

_____

_____

_____

_____

_____

_____

_____

_____

Date:
Location:

In a Nutshell: _____

_____

_____

More Details: _____

_____

_____

_____

_____

_____

_____

_____

Date:
Location:

In a Nutshell: _____

_____

_____

More Details: _____

_____

_____

_____

_____

_____

_____

_____

Date:

Location:

In a Nutshell: _____

_____

_____

More Details: _____

_____

_____

_____

_____

_____

_____

_____

Date:
Location:

In a Nutshell: _____

_____

_____

More Details: _____

_____

_____

_____

_____

_____

_____

_____

_____

Date:
Location:

In a Nutshell: _____

_____

_____

More Details: _____

_____

_____

_____

_____

_____

_____

_____

Date:

Location:

In a Nutshell: _____

_____

_____

More Details: _____

_____

_____

_____

_____

_____

_____

_____

Date:
Location:

In a Nutshell: _____

_____

_____

More Details: _____

_____

_____

_____

_____

_____

_____

_____

Date:
Location:

In a Nutshell: _____

_____

_____

More Details: _____

_____

_____

_____

_____

_____

_____

_____

Date:
Location:

In a Nutshell: _____

_____

_____

More Details: _____

_____

_____

_____

_____

_____

_____

_____

Date:
Location:

In a Nutshell: _____

_____

_____

More Details: _____

_____

_____

_____

_____

_____

_____

_____

Date:
Location:

In a Nutshell: _____

_____

_____

More Details: _____

_____

_____

_____

_____

_____

_____

_____

_____

Date:
Location:

In a Nutshell: _____

_____

_____

More Details: _____

_____

_____

_____

_____

_____

_____

_____

Date:
Location:

In a Nutshell: _____
_____

_____

More Details: _____
_____
_____
_____
_____
_____
_____
_____

Date:

Location:

In a Nutshell: _____

_____

_____

More Details: _____

_____

_____

_____

_____

_____

_____

_____

Date:
Location:

In a Nutshell: _____
_____
_____

More Details: _____
_____
_____
_____
_____
_____
_____
_____

Date:
Location:

In a Nutshell: _____

_____

_____

More Details: _____

_____

_____

_____

_____

_____

_____

_____

_____

Date:
Location:

In a Nutshell: _____

_____

_____

More Details: _____

_____

_____

_____

_____

_____

_____

_____

_____

Date:
Location:

In a Nutshell: _____

_____

_____

More Details: _____

_____

_____

_____

_____

_____

_____

_____

Date:

Location:

In a Nutshell: _____

_____

_____

More Details: _____

_____

_____

_____

_____

_____

_____

_____

Date:
Location:

In a Nutshell: _____

_____

_____

More Details: _____

_____

_____

_____

_____

_____

_____

_____

Date:
Location:

In a Nutshell: _____

_____

_____

More Details: _____

_____

_____

_____

_____

_____

_____

_____

Date:
Location:

In a Nutshell: _____
_____
_____

More Details: _____
_____
_____
_____
_____
_____
_____
_____

Date:
Location:

In a Nutshell: _____
_____
_____

More Details: _____
_____
_____
_____
_____
_____
_____
_____

Date:
Location:

In a Nutshell: _____
_____

_____

More Details: _____
_____
_____
_____
_____
_____
_____
_____
_____

Date:
Location:

In a Nutshell: _____

_____

_____

More Details: _____

_____

_____

_____

_____

_____

_____

_____

Date:

Location:

In a Nutshell: _____

_____

_____

More Details: _____

_____

_____

_____

_____

_____

_____

_____

Date:
Location:

In a Nutshell: _____

_____

_____

More Details: _____

_____

_____

_____

_____

_____

_____

_____

Date:
Location:

In a Nutshell: _____
_____
_____

More Details: _____
_____
_____
_____
_____
_____
_____
_____

Date:
Location:

In a Nutshell: _____

_____

_____

More Details: _____

_____

_____

_____

_____

_____

_____

_____

Date:

Location:

In a Nutshell: _____

_____

_____

More Details: _____

_____

_____

_____

_____

_____

_____

_____

_____

Date:
Location:

In a Nutshell: _____

_____

_____

More Details: _____

_____

_____

_____

_____

_____

_____

_____

_____

Date:
Location:

In a Nutshell: _____

_____

_____

More Details: _____

_____

_____

_____

_____

_____

_____

_____

_____

Date:
Location:

In a Nutshell: _____

_____

_____

More Details: _____

_____

_____

_____

_____

_____

_____

_____

_____

Date:
Location:

In a Nutshell: _____

_____

_____

More Details: _____

_____

_____

_____

_____

_____

_____

_____

Date:
Location:

In a Nutshell: _____

_____

_____

More Details: _____

_____

_____

_____

_____

_____

_____

_____

Date:
Location:

In a Nutshell: _____

_____

_____

More Details: _____

_____

_____

_____

_____

_____

_____

_____

_____

Date:
Location:

In a Nutshell: _____

_____

_____

More Details: _____

_____

_____

_____

_____

_____

_____

_____

Date:
Location:

In a Nutshell: _____

_____

_____

More Details: _____

_____

_____

_____

_____

_____

_____

_____

_____

Date:
Location:

In a Nutshell: _____
_____
_____

More Details: _____
_____
_____
_____
_____
_____
_____
_____

Date:
Location:

In a Nutshell: _____
_____
_____

More Details: _____
_____
_____
_____
_____
_____
_____
_____
_____

Date:
Location:

In a Nutshell: _____

_____

_____

More Details: _____

_____

_____

_____

_____

_____

_____

_____

Date:
Location:

In a Nutshell: _____

_____

_____

More Details: _____

_____

_____

_____

_____

_____

_____

_____

Date:
Location:

In a Nutshell: _____

_____

_____

More Details: _____

_____

_____

_____

_____

_____

_____

_____

Date:
Location:

In a Nutshell: _____

_____

_____

More Details: _____

_____

_____

_____

_____

_____

_____

_____

_____

Date:
Location:

In a Nutshell: _____

_____

_____

More Details: _____

_____

_____

_____

_____

_____

_____

_____

Date:

Location:

In a Nutshell: _____

_____

_____

More Details: _____

_____

_____

_____

_____

_____

_____

_____

Date:
Location:

In a Nutshell: _____

_____

_____

More Details: _____

_____

_____

_____

_____

_____

_____

_____

Date:
Location:

In a Nutshell: _____

_____

_____

More Details: _____

_____

_____

_____

_____

_____

_____

_____

_____

Date:
Location:

In a Nutshell: _____

_____

_____

More Details: _____

_____

_____

_____

_____

_____

_____

_____

Date:
Location:

In a Nutshell: _____
_____
_____

More Details: _____
_____
_____
_____
_____
_____
_____
_____
_____

Date:
Location:

In a Nutshell: _____
_____
_____

More Details: _____
_____
_____
_____
_____
_____
_____
_____
_____

Date:
Location:

In a Nutshell: _____

_____

_____

More Details: _____

_____

_____

_____

_____

_____

_____

_____

Date:
Location:

In a Nutshell: _____

_____

_____

More Details: _____

_____

_____

_____

_____

_____

_____

_____

Date:
Location:

In a Nutshell: _____

_____

_____

More Details: _____

_____

_____

_____

_____

_____

_____

_____

_____

Date:
Location:

In a Nutshell: _____

_____

_____

More Details: _____

_____

_____

_____

_____

_____

_____

_____

Date:

Location:

In a Nutshell: _____

_____

_____

More Details: _____

_____

_____

_____

_____

_____

_____

_____

_____

Date:

Location:

In a Nutshell: _____

_____

_____

More Details: _____

_____

_____

_____

_____

_____

_____

_____

Date:

Location:

In a Nutshell: _____

_____

_____

More Details: _____

_____

_____

_____

_____

_____

_____

_____

Date:
Location:

In a Nutshell: _____

_____

_____

More Details: _____

_____

_____

_____

_____

_____

_____

_____

Date:

Location:

In a Nutshell: _____

_____

_____

More Details: _____

_____

_____

_____

_____

_____

_____

_____

Date:
Location:

In a Nutshell: _____

_____

_____

More Details: _____

_____

_____

_____

_____

_____

_____

_____

Date:
Location:

In a Nutshell: _____

_____

_____

More Details: _____

_____

_____

_____

_____

_____

_____

_____

Date:
Location:

In a Nutshell: _____

_____

_____

More Details: _____

_____

_____

_____

_____

_____

_____

_____

Date:
Location:

In a Nutshell: _____

_____

_____

More Details: _____

_____

_____

_____

_____

_____

_____

_____

Date:
Location:

In a Nutshell: _____

_____

_____

More Details: _____

_____

_____

_____

_____

_____

_____

_____

Date:
Location:

In a Nutshell: _____

_____

_____

More Details: _____

_____

_____

_____

_____

_____

_____

_____

_____

Date:
Location:

In a Nutshell: _____
_____
_____

More Details: _____
_____
_____
_____
_____
_____
_____
_____

Date:
Location:

In a Nutshell: _____
_____
_____

More Details: _____
_____
_____
_____
_____
_____
_____
_____
_____

Date:
Location:

In a Nutshell: _____

_____

_____

More Details: _____

_____

_____

_____

_____

_____

_____

_____

_____

Date:
Location:

In a Nutshell: _____

_____

_____

More Details: _____

_____

_____

_____

_____

_____

_____

_____

_____

Date:
Location:

In a Nutshell: _____

_____

_____

More Details: _____

_____

_____

_____

_____

_____

_____

_____

Date:
Location:

In a Nutshell: _____

_____

_____

More Details: _____

_____

_____

_____

_____

_____

_____

_____

Date:
Location:

In a Nutshell: _____
_____
_____

More Details: _____
_____
_____
_____
_____
_____
_____
_____
_____

Date:
Location:

In a Nutshell: _____

_____

_____

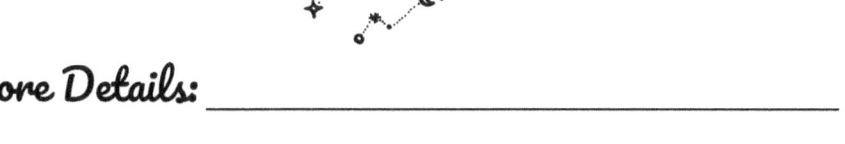

More Details: _____

_____

_____

_____

_____

_____

_____

_____

_____

Date:
Location:

In a Nutshell: _____
_____
_____

More Details: _____
_____
_____
_____
_____
_____
_____
_____
_____

Date:
Location:

In a Nutshell: _____

_____

_____

More Details: _____

_____

_____

_____

_____

_____

_____

_____

Date:
Location:

In a Nutshell: _____

_____

_____

More Details: _____

_____

_____

_____

_____

_____

_____

_____

_____

Date:

Location:

In a Nutshell: _____

_____

_____

More Details: _____

_____

_____

_____

_____

_____

_____

_____

_____

Date:
Location:

In a Nutshell: _____

_____

_____

More Details: _____

_____

_____

_____

_____

_____

_____

_____

Date:
Location:

In a Nutshell: _____

_____

_____

More Details: _____

_____

_____

_____

_____

_____

_____

_____

Date:
Location:

In a Nutshell: _____

_____

_____

More Details: _____

_____

_____

_____

_____

_____

_____

_____

Date:
Location:

In a Nutshell: _____
_____
_____

More Details: _____
_____
_____
_____
_____
_____
_____
_____

Date:
Location:

In a Nutshell: _____
_____
_____

More Details: _____
_____
_____
_____
_____
_____
_____
_____
_____

Date:
Location:

In a Nutshell: _____

_____

_____

More Details: _____

_____

_____

_____

_____

_____

_____

_____

_____

Date:
Location:

In a Nutshell: _____

_____

_____

More Details: _____

_____

_____

_____

_____

_____

_____

_____

_____

Date:
Location:

In a Nutshell: _____
_____
_____

More Details: _____
_____
_____
_____
_____
_____
_____
_____
_____

Date:
Location:

In a Nutshell: _____

_____

_____

More Details: _____

_____

_____

_____

_____

_____

_____

_____

Date:

Location:

In a Nutshell: _____

_____

_____

More Details: _____

_____

_____

_____

_____

_____

_____

_____

_____

Date:
Location:

In a Nutshell: _____
_____
_____

More Details: _____
_____
_____
_____
_____
_____
_____
_____
_____

Date:

Location:

In a Nutshell: _____

_____

_____

More Details: _____

_____

_____

_____

_____

_____

_____

_____

Date:
Location:

In a Nutshell: _____

_____

_____

More Details: _____

_____

_____

_____

_____

_____

_____

_____

_____

Date:
Location:

In a Nutshell: _____

_____

_____

More Details: _____

_____

_____

_____

_____

_____

_____

_____

Date:

Location:

In a Nutshell: _____

_____

_____

More Details: _____

_____

_____

_____

_____

_____

_____

_____

Date:
Location:

In a Nutshell: _____
_____
_____

More Details: _____
_____
_____
_____
_____
_____
_____
_____

Date:
Location:

In a Nutshell: _____
_____
_____

More Details: _____
_____
_____
_____
_____
_____
_____
_____

Date:

Location:

In a Nutshell: _____

_____

_____

More Details: _____

_____

_____

_____

_____

_____

_____

_____

Date:
Location:

In a Nutshell: _____

_____

_____

More Details: _____

_____

_____

_____

_____

_____

_____

_____

Date:
Location:

In a Nutshell: _____

_____

_____

More Details: _____

_____

_____

_____

_____

_____

_____

_____

Date:
Location:

In a Nutshell: _____
_____
_____

More Details: _____
_____
_____
_____
_____
_____
_____
_____
_____

Date:

Location:

In a Nutshell: _____

_____

_____

More Details: _____

_____

_____

_____

_____

_____

_____

_____

_____

Date:
Location:

In a Nutshell: _____

_____

_____

More Details: _____

_____

_____

_____

_____

_____

_____

_____

_____

Date:
Location:

In a Nutshell: _____

_____

_____

More Details: _____

_____

_____

_____

_____

_____

_____

_____

Date:

Location:

In a Nutshell: _____

_____

_____

More Details: _____

_____

_____

_____

_____

_____

_____

_____

_____

Date:
Location:

In a Nutshell: _____

_____

_____

More Details: _____

_____

_____

_____

_____

_____

_____

_____

_____

Date:
Location:

In a Nutshell: _____

_____

_____

More Details: _____

_____

_____

_____

_____

_____

_____

_____

Date:
Location:

In a Nutshell: _____

_____

_____

More Details: _____

_____

_____

_____

_____

_____

_____

_____

_____

Date:

Location:

In a Nutshell: _____

_____

_____

More Details: _____

_____

_____

_____

_____

_____

_____

_____

Date:

Location:

In a Nutshell: _____

_____

_____

More Details: _____

_____

_____

_____

_____

_____

_____

_____

Date:
Location:

In a Nutshell: _____

_____

_____

More Details: _____

_____

_____

_____

_____

_____

_____

_____

Date:
Location:

In a Nutshell: _____

_____

_____

More Details: _____

_____

_____

_____

_____

_____

_____

_____

Date:

Location:

In a Nutshell: _____

_____

_____

More Details: _____

_____

_____

_____

_____

_____

_____

_____

_____

Date:

Location:

In a Nutshell: _____

_____

_____

More Details: _____

_____

_____

_____

_____

_____

_____

_____

Date:
Location:

In a Nutshell: _____

_____

_____

More Details: _____

_____

_____

_____

_____

_____

_____

_____

Date:

Location:

In a Nutshell: _____

_____

_____

More Details: _____

_____

_____

_____

_____

_____

_____

_____

_____

Date:
Location:

In a Nutshell: _____

_____

_____

More Details: _____

_____

_____

_____

_____

_____

_____

_____

Date:
Location:

In a Nutshell: _____

_____

_____

More Details: _____

_____

_____

_____

_____

_____

_____

_____

Date:
Location:

In a Nutshell: _____

_____

_____

More Details: _____

_____

_____

_____

_____

_____

_____

_____

Date:
Location:

In a Nutshell: _____

_____

_____

More Details: _____

_____

_____

_____

_____

_____

_____

_____

Date:
Location:

In a Nutshell: _____

_____

_____

More Details: _____

_____

_____

_____

_____

_____

_____

_____

Date:
Location:

In a Nutshell: _____

_____

_____

More Details: _____

_____

_____

_____

_____

_____

_____

_____

Date:

Location:

In a Nutshell: _____

_____

_____

More Details: _____

_____

_____

_____

_____

_____

_____

_____

_____

Date:
Location:

In a Nutshell: _____

_____

_____

More Details: _____

_____

_____

_____

_____

_____

_____

_____

Date:

Location:

In a Nutshell: _____

_____

_____

More Details: _____

_____

_____

_____

_____

_____

_____

_____

Date:

Location:

In a Nutshell: _____

_____

_____

More Details: _____

_____

_____

_____

_____

_____

_____

_____

_____

Date:
Location:

In a Nutshell: _____
_____
_____

More Details: _____
_____
_____
_____
_____
_____
_____
_____
_____

Date:
Location:

In a Nutshell: _____
_____
_____

More Details: _____
_____
_____
_____
_____
_____
_____
_____
_____

Date:
Location:

In a Nutshell: _____
_____
_____

More Details: _____
_____
_____
_____
_____
_____
_____
_____

Date:
Location:

In a Nutshell: _____

_____

_____

More Details: _____

_____

_____

_____

_____

_____

_____

_____

_____

Date:

Location:

In a Nutshell: _____

_____

_____

More Details: _____

_____

_____

_____

_____

_____

_____

_____

_____

Date:

Location:

In a Nutshell: _____

_____

_____

More Details: _____

_____

_____

_____

_____

_____

_____

_____

_____

Date:
Location:

In a Nutshell: _____
_____
_____

More Details: _____
_____
_____
_____
_____
_____
_____
_____

Date:
Location:

In a Nutshell: _____

_____

_____

More Details: _____

_____

_____

_____

_____

_____

_____

_____

Date:

Location:

In a Nutshell: _____

_____

_____

More Details: _____

_____

_____

_____

_____

_____

_____

_____

Date:
Location:

In a Nutshell: _____
_____
_____

More Details: _____
_____
_____
_____
_____
_____
_____
_____
_____

Date:
Location:

In a Nutshell: _____

_____

_____

More Details: _____

_____

_____

_____

_____

_____

_____

_____

_____

Date:
Location:

In a Nutshell: _____

_____

_____

More Details: _____

_____

_____

_____

_____

_____

_____

_____

_____

Date:
Location:

In a Nutshell: _____

_____

_____

More Details: _____

_____

_____

_____

_____

_____

_____

_____

_____

Date:
Location:

In a Nutshell: _____

_____

_____

More Details: _____

_____

_____

_____

_____

_____

_____

_____

_____

Date:
Location:

In a Nutshell: _____

_____

_____

More Details: _____

_____

_____

_____

_____

_____

_____

_____

Date:
Location:

In a Nutshell: _____

_____

_____

More Details: _____

_____

_____

_____

_____

_____

_____

_____

_____

Date:
Location:

In a Nutshell: _____

_____

_____

More Details: _____

_____

_____

_____

_____

_____

_____

_____

Date:
Location:

In a Nutshell: _____

_____

_____

More Details: _____

_____

_____

_____

_____

_____

_____

_____

_____

Date:
Location:

In a Nutshell: _____

_____

_____

More Details: _____

_____

_____

_____

_____

_____

_____

_____

Date:
Location:

In a Nutshell: _____

_____

_____

More Details: _____

_____

_____

_____

_____

_____

_____

_____

Date:
Location:

In a Nutshell: _____
_____
_____

More Details: _____
_____
_____
_____
_____
_____
_____
_____

Date:
Location:

In a Nutshell: _____
_____
_____

More Details: _____
_____
_____
_____
_____
_____
_____
_____
_____

Date:
Location:

In a Nutshell: _____

_____

_____

More Details: _____

_____

_____

_____

_____

_____

_____

_____

Date:
Location:

In a Nutshell: _____

_____

_____

More Details: _____

_____

_____

_____

_____

_____

_____

_____

Date:
Location:

In a Nutshell: _____

_____

_____

More Details: _____

_____

_____

_____

_____

_____

_____

_____

Date:
Location:

In a Nutshell: _____

_____

_____

More Details: _____

_____

_____

_____

_____

_____

_____

_____

Date:
Location:

In a Nutshell: _____
_____
_____

More Details: _____
_____
_____
_____
_____
_____
_____
_____

Date:
Location:

In a Nutshell: _____
_____
_____

More Details: _____
_____
_____
_____
_____
_____
_____
_____
_____

Date:
Location:

In a Nutshell: _____

_____

_____

More Details: _____

_____

_____

_____

_____

_____

_____

_____

_____

Date:
Location:

In a Nutshell: _____
_____
_____

More Details: _____
_____
_____
_____
_____
_____
_____
_____
_____

Date:
Location:

In a Nutshell: _____

_____

_____

More Details: _____

_____

_____

_____

_____

_____

_____

_____

Date:
Location:

In a Nutshell: _____

_____

_____

More Details: _____

_____

_____

_____

_____

_____

_____

_____

Date:
Location:

In a Nutshell: _____
_____
_____

More Details: _____
_____
_____
_____
_____
_____
_____
_____

Date:
Location:

In a Nutshell: _____

_____

_____

More Details: _____

_____

_____

_____

_____

_____

_____

_____

Date:
Location:

In a Nutshell: _____

_____

_____

More Details: _____

_____

_____

_____

_____

_____

_____

_____

Date:

Location:

In a Nutshell: _____

_____

_____

More Details: _____

_____

_____

_____

_____

_____

_____

_____

_____

Date:
Location:

In a Nutshell: _____

_____

_____

More Details: _____

_____

_____

_____

_____

_____

_____

_____

Date:

Location:

In a Nutshell: _____

_____

_____

More Details: _____

_____

_____

_____

_____

_____

_____

_____

_____

Date:
Location:

In a Nutshell: _____
_____
_____

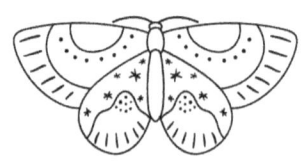

More Details: _____
_____
_____
_____
_____
_____
_____
_____

Date:
Location:

In a Nutshell: _____

_____

_____

More Details: _____

_____

_____

_____

_____

_____

_____

_____

Date:
Location:

In a Nutshell: _____
_____
_____

More Details: _____
_____
_____
_____
_____
_____
_____
_____
_____

Date:
Location:

In a Nutshell: _____
_____
_____

More Details: _____
_____
_____
_____
_____
_____
_____
_____
_____

Date:
Location:

In a Nutshell: _____
_____
_____

More Details: _____
_____
_____
_____
_____
_____
_____
_____

Date:

Location:

In a Nutshell: _____

_____

_____

More Details: _____

_____

_____

_____

_____

_____

_____

_____

_____

Date:
Location:

In a Nutshell: _____

_____

_____

More Details: _____

_____

_____

_____

_____

_____

_____

_____

Date:
Location:

In a Nutshell: _____
_____
_____

More Details: _____
_____
_____
_____
_____
_____
_____
_____
_____

Date:
Location:

In a Nutshell: _____
_____
_____

More Details: _____
_____
_____
_____
_____
_____
_____
_____

Date:

Location:

In a Nutshell: _____

_____

_____

More Details: _____

_____

_____

_____

_____

_____

_____

_____

Date:

Location:

In a Nutshell: _____

_____

_____

More Details: _____

_____

_____

_____

_____

_____

_____

_____

Date:

Location:

In a Nutshell: _____

_____

_____

More Details: _____

_____

_____

_____

_____

_____

_____

_____

Date:
Location:

In a Nutshell: _____
_____
_____

More Details: _____
_____
_____
_____
_____
_____
_____
_____
_____

Date:

Location:

In a Nutshell: _____

_____

_____

More Details: _____

_____

_____

_____

_____

_____

_____

_____

_____

Date:
Location:

In a Nutshell: _____

_____

_____

More Details: _____

_____

_____

_____

_____

_____

_____

_____

Date:
Location:

In a Nutshell: _____

_____

_____

More Details: _____

_____

_____

_____

_____

_____

_____

_____

_____

Date:

Location:

In a Nutshell: _____

_____

_____

More Details: _____

_____

_____

_____

_____

_____

_____

_____

Date:

Location:

In a Nutshell: _____

_____

_____

More Details: _____

_____

_____

_____

_____

_____

_____

_____

_____

Date:
Location:

In a Nutshell: _____
_____
_____

More Details: _____
_____
_____
_____
_____
_____
_____
_____
_____

Date:

Location:

In a Nutshell: _____

_____

_____

More Details: _____

_____

_____

_____

_____

_____

_____

_____

Date:
Location:

In a Nutshell: _____

_____

_____

More Details: _____

_____

_____

_____

_____

_____

_____

_____

Date:
Location:

In a Nutshell: _____
_____
_____

More Details: _____
_____
_____
_____
_____
_____
_____
_____
_____

Date:
Location:

In a Nutshell: _____
_____
_____

More Details: _____
_____
_____
_____
_____
_____
_____
_____
_____

Date:
Location:

In a Nutshell: _____

_____

_____

More Details: _____

_____

_____

_____

_____

_____

_____

_____

Date:
Location:

In a Nutshell: _____

_____

_____

More Details: _____

_____

_____

_____

_____

_____

_____

_____

Date:
Location:

In a Nutshell: _____

_____

_____

More Details: _____

_____

_____

_____

_____

_____

_____

_____

_____

Date:

Location:

In a Nutshell: _____

_____

_____

More Details: _____

_____

_____

_____

_____

_____

_____

_____

Date:
Location:

In a Nutshell: _____
_____
_____

More Details: _____
_____
_____
_____
_____
_____
_____
_____

Date:

Location:

In a Nutshell: _____

_____

_____

More Details: _____

_____

_____

_____

_____

_____

_____

_____

Date:

Location:

In a Nutshell: _____

_____

_____

More Details: _____

_____

_____

_____

_____

_____

_____

_____

Date:
Location:

In a Nutshell: _____

_____

_____

More Details: _____

_____

_____

_____

_____

_____

_____

_____

Date:
Location:

In a Nutshell: _____

_____

_____

More Details: _____

_____

_____

_____

_____

_____

_____

_____

Date:

Location:

In a Nutshell: _____

_____

_____

More Details: _____

_____

_____

_____

_____

_____

_____

_____

Date:

Location:

In a Nutshell: _____

_____

_____

More Details: _____

_____

_____

_____

_____

_____

_____

_____

_____

Date:
Location:

In a Nutshell: _____

_____

_____

More Details: _____

_____

_____

_____

_____

_____

_____

_____

Date:
Location:

In a Nutshell: _____

_____

_____

More Details: _____

_____

_____

_____

_____

_____

_____

_____

Date:

Location:

In a Nutshell: _____

_____

_____

More Details: _____

_____

_____

_____

_____

_____

_____

_____

_____

Date:

Location:

In a Nutshell: _____

_____

_____

More Details: _____

_____

_____

_____

_____

_____

_____

_____

Date:
Location:

In a Nutshell: _____

_____

_____

More Details: _____

_____

_____

_____

_____

_____

_____

_____

_____

Date:
Location:

In a Nutshell: _____
_____
_____

More Details: _____
_____
_____
_____
_____
_____
_____
_____
_____

Date:
Location:

In a Nutshell: _____

_____

_____

More Details: _____

_____

_____

_____

_____

_____

_____

_____

Date:
Location:

In a Nutshell: _____

_____

_____

More Details: _____

_____

_____

_____

_____

_____

_____

_____

_____

Date:
Location:

In a Nutshell: _____

_____

_____

More Details: _____

_____

_____

_____

_____

_____

_____

_____

Congratulations: you've finished your book!

For next year's journal or information on her many cozy fantasy books, find Elle Hartford on Etsy, social media, or her website, ellehartford.com.

www.ingramcontent.com/pod-product-compliance
Lightning Source LLC
Chambersburg PA
CBHW050445150626
46551CB00029B/1700